Introducing Solids & Making Your Own Organic Baby Food

A Step-by-Step Guide to Weaning Baby off Breast & Starting Solids. Delicious, Easy-to-Make, & Healthy Homemade Baby Food Recipes Included.

Katherine Smiley

Copyright© 2014 by Katherine Smiley

Introducing Solids & Making Your Own Organic Baby Food

Publisher: Enlightened Publishing

ISBN-13: 978-1500496999

ISBN-10: 1500496995

Disclaimer

The Publisher has strived to be as accurate and complete as possible in the creation of this book. While all attempts have been made to verify information provided in this publication, the Publisher assumes no responsibility for errors, omissions, or contrary interpretation of the subject matter herein. Any perceived slights of specific persons, peoples, or organizations are unintentional.

This book is not intended for use as a source of legal, business, accounting or financial advice. All readers are advised to seek services of competent professionals in the legal, business, accounting, and finance fields.

The information in this book is not intended or implied to be a substitute for professional medical advice, diagnosis or treatment. All content contained in this book is for general information purposes only. Always consult your healthcare provider before carrying on any health program.

Table of Contents

Introduction

Taylor's story: Taylor is a healthy 6 month old who is underweight for her age. She has been exclusively breastfed and mom wants to introduce solids along with breast milk now that Taylor is 6 months old.

Jason's story: Jason is five months of age and robust in weight. His parents report he drinks twelve bottles a day and doesn't seem satisfied. He is curious about what mom and dad are eating but hasn't eaten solid foods yet.

Marie's story: Marie was premature by 2 months and is now 6 months of age. She drinks 8 bottles a day and seems satisfied. She is not showing any interest in the feeding of others.

The point of these vignettes is to say that every baby is different and what works with one baby may not work well with another baby. There are babies that are perfectly ready to eat solid foods by five months of age and actually seem to need the extra calories they didn't get from bottled formula. There are babies that have received all their nutrition from mother's milk and may take some extra time learning how to eat from a spoon. There are babies with health problems or problems with prematurity that may need the doctor's advice as to when be the best time to start solid foods.

Breast is Best

Most pediatricians will tell parents that until the child reaches the age of six months, he or she should be exclusively breast fed on demand. This means that when the baby cries or indicates the need to feed, the mother will breastfeed the child until the child is satisfied.

Mothers who work or who can't breastfeed for some reason should find a good formula for the baby. Most formulas are basically the same and include cow's milk-based formula, soy-formula, and formula that contains elemental formulas for baby's with allergies or digestive problems. These are the formulas your baby might be on at the time of weaning:

- **Soy Formulas**. These are for babies that might be allergic to the proteins in cow's milk. They come in several brands, including Similac Isomil Advance, Enfamil ProSobee Lipil, Nestle Good Start Supreme DHA & ARA Soy and Earth's Best Organic Soy Infant Formula with DHA and ARA.

- **Nutramigen Lipil and Alimentum Advance**. These contain basic, hydrolyzed proteins for babies with multiple allergies or for babies with colic.

- **Milk-based Formulas**. This is the type of formula most babies can take and are the most used formulas available. They include Enfamil AR Lipil, Enfamil ProSobee LIPIL, Enfamil Gentlease, Enfamil LactoFree LIPIL, Nestle Good Start ARA and DHA, Similac Advance, Similac Advance Early Shield, Similac Lactose Free Advance and Similac Sensitive.

What are ARA and DHA?

Many baby formulas now contain ARA and DHA as special additives. These are substances found in breast milk and seem to be helpful in the growth of the brain and eyes in newborns and young infants. DHA is also called docohexaenoic acid, while ARA is also known as arachidonic acid. These are essential fatty acids that can't be synthesized by the body but must be present in the food you eat.

Formula makers realized that breast milk contained these important molecules and started adding them to most formulas. While the addition of these molecules doesn't make baby formula exactly the same as breast milk, it does make these formulas a closer match to breast milk than ever before. Only Nestle Good Start without DHA or ARA is available without the fatty acids but you have to buy it online.

The Babies

The babies outlined above are facing the time for weaning. Taylor may have trouble dealing with food that comes from a spoon because she has been exclusively breastfed.

Jason's mom might want to talk to the pediatrician about starting Jason early because he's unable to get enough calories from milk alone. Marie might best be a couple of months away from starting solids. While her chronological age is 6 months, her actual age is more like 4 months because she was preterm. Her doctor might recommend that she start solid foods at 7-8 months.

Whenever you as parents and your doctor decide on the right time to start solids, you need to be prepared to feed your baby healthy organic food, to teach the baby how to use utensils when the time comes, and to deal with issues like picky eating and food allergies. Every baby truly is different in his likes and dislikes around feeding. Some will eat just about anything and consume a large amount. Others will refuse to eat certain foods and will eat only small amounts of food at a time.

Weaning a baby should be interesting and fun. Always remember that the baby will still receive much of his or her nutrition from baby formula or breast milk so you get the opportunity to experiment with what your baby likes and what he doesn't like.

In this book, we will talk about how to wean a baby, what foods to choose and how to make some really healthy organic baby foods for your baby to dine on. The process of weaning will take several months of trying and testing different foods. Soon, you'll have a collection of organic foods that will be available for mealtime. We'll also talk about some troubles you might have with weaning your baby. Every baby gets weaned sometime and will soon have a variety of foods that match your own at the supper table.

Chapter 1: What a Baby Needs to Eat

The first thing your baby needs to eat is calories. Calories provide energy and allow your baby to gain weight. Because of their need for weight gain, babies need a relatively higher number of calories when compared to adults. For babies under six months, they need about 50-55 calories per pound of body weight. Bear in mind that formula, recommended before the age of six months is 20 calories per ounce.

Babies from six months to a year will need about 45 calories per pound of body weight. Babies will double their birth weight at 6 months and triple their birth weight at a year of age. The National Academy of Sciences recommends to parents and doctors that babies under six months of age receive half of their calories from fat. Between seven and 12 months of age, the baby should receive 35 to 40 percent of their calories from fat.

Truly, babies are growing all the time. In order to triple their body weight at the time of their third birthday, they need to eat a lot of food and they need to eat often. Feeding helps babies grow physically, mentally, emotionally and socially. Food and eating are social behaviors and children learn a lot by watching others eat and mimicking the behaviors of others.

Nutritional Needs for Babies

From birth to four months the baby only needs breast milk or formula. Some babies get a combination of the two. Babies at this stage are fed on demand. It involves the mother figuring out which of the babies several cries means "I'm hungry" and feeding the baby until he or she is full. Breastfeeding mothers sometimes wonder if their baby is getting enough. In such cases, she needs to look at how comfortable the child is after feeding, how far apart the feedings are and, most importantly, how much weight the baby is gaining. If the baby is gaining an appropriate amount of weight at his or her well baby visits, there is no need to be concerned.

At this stage, some babies eat a couple of ounces every two hours while other babies will get four ounces in every four hours. It just depends on the baby and his or her habits of eating. Feeding your baby on demand builds trust and teaches the baby that someone is always there for him. Babies tend to take in between 16 and 32 ounces of breast milk or formula during the first four months. If you feed your baby formula, try to stick to the same one as long as it appears the baby has no allergies or intolerance to the formula.

At between four to six months, it will be apparent that your infant is interested in food. He or she may grab at your spoon or "taste" some food off the end of your utensil. It may also seem like you are breastfeeding more frequently than before and that your baby just isn't getting enough. Your baby may wake up more frequently during the night than before because of hunger. He will be able to sit up and hold his head on his own so that the process of feeding solids will be easier. He will develop a palmar grasp, meaning that he can hold things and bring them to his mouth. Your baby will show he or she is hungry by leaning toward the spoon or may push away foods he doesn't like or when he is full. There is a solid communication around eating and you and your baby will be part of that communication.

Your baby will receive about half of his nutrients from formula or breast milk and about half from solid foods. Ideally, your baby should eat organic foods that are free of pesticides, hormones, and other chemicals. A good first choice is rice cereal fortified with iron. The reason you need to give your baby supplemental iron is because his or her iron stores are dropping to lower levels than in the newborn stage and the rice cereal fortified with iron will help build up the iron stores. Rice cereal is mixed with formula or breast milk so it will have a nice balance of protein, calories, carbohydrates and fat.

When you advance the babies diet, consider the following things:

- What nutrients the baby needs

- The readiness of the baby to eat the food in question

- Whether or not your baby has allergies to the food or a related food

Right after introducing rice cereal successfully, you'll want to enrich your baby's diet with vitamins C and A. This means foods like applesauce, dark green vegetable, deep orange vegetable (pureed carrots or squash). Foods are added one at a time, not mixing foods until about three days have passed so you know there is no allergy going on.

Actual Nutrient Requirements from Birth to Six Months

Just like adults have nutrient requirements, so does your baby. These are the major vitamins and minerals your baby needs:

- Protein, 13 grams per day
- Iron, 6 grams per day
- Calcium 400 milligrams per day
- Vitamin A 375 IU per day
- Vitamin C, 30 mg per day

What Baby Needs When

- At 4-6 months, you start with single grain cereals, beginning with rice cereal and transitioning to oatmeal. These are fortified with iron and are mixed with baby formula or breast milk. It may taste horrible to you but babies love it. It does not need to be sweetened with sugar or any other kind of baby food, especially in the beginning.

- At 6-8 months, you can begin to give your baby strained or pureed fruits such as prunes, applesauce, pears, or bananas. All food should be organically grown, cooked and pureed with a blender or mashed with a masher. It should be watery at first, until the baby tolerated thicker foods.

- 7-8 months is a good time to give your baby pureed or strained organic vegetables like carrots, squash, peas, potatoes and avocados. All vegetables should be organically grown and washed. They can be baked, boiled or steamed until soft and then pureed with a blender or food processor. You can make it more liquid by adding breast milk, water or baby formula. The food can be thicker as your child grows.

- At 7-8 months, your baby needs protein. This means cutting up or pureeing small pieces of meat like chicken, turkey, boneless fish, or beans like black beans, red beans or pinto beans.

- At 8-10 months, you can get away with mashing organic fruits and vegetables. The food doesn't have to be pureed anymore but can simply be mashed until soft. Baby should have some teeth by now but if he doesn't, he can chew with his gums.

- At 8-10 months, you can use oat cereal pieces and other pieces of finger food. The finger food must be cut up so your baby can swallow it without choking. Teething crackers are good as are small pieces of whole grain pasta.

- At 8-10 months, you can give small amounts of yogurt, cottage cheese or small chunks of cheese that the baby picks up and chews. This might be the time to teach your baby how to use a spoon to get as much food as possible on the spoon.

- At 8-10 months, you can scramble eggs and give them in cut up pieces to the baby.

- At 10-12 months, the baby can begin eating the same food you are eating as long as it is cut up in the proper chunks so the baby can easily chew and swallow it. Watch how your baby chews to make sure he or she is chewing and swallowing adequately.

Like you, your baby will have certain dietary needs and certain caloric needs. As long as you keep within certain guidelines and feed your child the foods he or she can tolerate and consume, your baby should have a healthy diet. Once you know your baby doesn't have an allergy to a food, you can give the baby a variety of foods—even 2-3 different foods per meal. Your baby will learn to love the variety and will get more nutrients out of a varied diet.

Chapter 2: Nutrition in Jarred Baby Food

As parents, we expect that our baby foods to be as nutritious as possible. It turns out that jarred baby food isn't as nutritious as once thought. In fact, some baby foods are diluted with non-nutritive substances. The only reason they don't result in harm to the baby is because they still receive much of their nutrition from breast milk or formula.

Both Heinz and Gerber replace real food your baby would eat with water and thickening agents. This makes jarred baby food nutritionally inferior to food you'd make yourself for your baby. The single ingredient foods made by baby food companies differ slightly because of the amount of water and thickener added to the foods. Gerber and Heinz add the most. The thickening agents are usually flour-based or are chemically modified starches and are added to more than half of their twenty five most popular fruits, mixed vegetables, desserts and dinners for babies over six months of age.

As parents, you're paying for fillers as well as real food and you're getting an inferior product that doesn't contain all the nutrients homemade foods have in them. On the good side, most of the products by Beech-Nut and Earth's best contain fewer fillers. Baby foods are expensive per ounce when compared to the same foods designed for adults. You often pay more than double per ounce for something like carrots that can be easily boiled or steamed and mashed for baby. Baby fruit juices are double the price of regular juices and things like canned diced carrots are much more expensive if you buy them as a "baby product".

Makers of baby foods create a mystique about their products to confuse parents into thinking it's something they couldn't duplicate at home. Parents are victims of advertising campaigns indicating that baby food companies have the best in nutrition; these are falsehoods that parents need to recognize and learn how to give baby truly healthy foods. A food processor, blender, or even forks are all that is necessary to give baby the texture he needs and the nutrition he needs.

Recent research indicates that parents should do their best to prepare baby food at home with well cooked foods (except bananas) that are of a texture that fits with baby's needs at the age the baby is at. If you buy baby food, read the ingredients. Avoid baby food that has added sugar, modified food starch, rice, wheat or other flours. Single foods should contain just the food and water as ingredients. Choose the brand that has the most calories because this has the least amount of added water. The brand "Growing Healthy" is one of the most expensive but it has more nutrition in the single foods when compared to other brands. Gerber and Heinz meat and vegetable or meat and fruit combos don't contain any fillers so they're more nutritious than similar foods with fillers. Earth's Best is organic but that can't be proven. Other brands may be just as "organic" as Earth's Best.

Avoid giving your baby infant desserts. Choose plain fruit baby food instead or buy unsweetened apple sauces or similar fruit sauces to avoid giving the baby the idea that sweet is best. Just know that there is nothing magical about jarred baby foods that warrant the high prices you pay for them. They aren't even very nutritious.

As parents, we need to hold the baby food industry accountable and let them know we want them to replace starches with real food and remove added sugar and salt. They need to stop making baby desserts and lower the prices to comparable adult foods. Supermarkets could help by making and marketing their own brands of cheaper baby foods.

As for the government, the US Food and Drug Administration should propose legislation to require truth in advertising when it comes to baby foods. All fillers and added products in baby food should be on the label. Deceptive advertising such as saying a baby food is "tapioca" should be changed to say "contains chemically modified food starch". The labeling as to what's in the baby food should be easily readable and not in tiny print no one can read.

Chapter 3: Weaning a Baby to Solids

Your baby is four to six months old. Is she ready to eat solids? How do we start them? What do we start with? These are questions we'll answer in this chapter. You need to know first that if you don't want to start solids until your baby is 6 months old, it will be just fine. The baby has all the nutrition he or she needs for the first six months just drinking breast milk or baby formula. At six months of age, not only will the baby be ready for solid foods but it is time to open the baby up to getting nutritious foods in different ways.

Every baby is different and some babies will be ready as early as 4 months to feed. Talk to your doctor if you think that your baby is ready earlier than 6 months of age. Solids should be introduced no sooner than 17 weeks after the baby was supposed to be due. Your baby's immune system and digestive system need to be prepared to consume food other than formula or breast milk.

Signs that Your Baby is Ready for Solids

- Your baby feeds formula or breast milk more often or during the night

- Your baby seems hungry even after feeding completely

- Your baby was sleeping during the night and is now awakening to feed

- Your baby shows interest in your eating

- Your baby can hold his or her head up by himself

- Your baby has lost the "stick out her tongue" reflex that would just force food out

Up to age one year, your baby will still be drinking up to 20 ounces of breast milk or formula per day so don't cut down on these feedings just because the baby will be starting solid foods. Milk is still a major part of your child's diet so keep it up. You can use a small amount of cow's milk to prepare solid foods or in other recipes but it shouldn't replace formula or breast milk until the baby is a year of age. You should always use pasteurized, full fat (whole) milk whenever you feed your baby cow's milk.

The First Feedings

If you go by traditional methods of weaning a baby, the first several feedings involve a tablespoon or two of very runny food. As mentioned, many parents start with rice cereal mixed with enough breast milk or formula to make the meal runny enough to spoon in a baby spoonful at a time. Don't worry about drips or messes as the baby doesn't have the ability to neatly take in food and swallow it.

Other choices of food as your baby becomes accustomed to rice cereal are oat cereal, pureed or mashed cooked vegetables, mashed or pureed fruits, maize, or potato. By the time your baby is ten months old, you can try rice, bread, crackers and pasta. Milk and dairy foods like yogurt can be tried at about ten to twelve months as can meat, fish, eggs and beans. If you mix up the types of food your baby eats, he or she will be less of a picky eater. Make sure you switch from savory to sweet foods as often as possible so your baby doesn't develop a sweet tooth. Babies should like all kinds of food.

Expect that your baby will eat very small portions in the beginning. This means just a tablespoon or two three times per day. You should still be breastfeeding on demand or giving the baby 500-600 ml of baby formula per day. Use a coated baby spoon or plastic spoon in the beginning. Some companies make a wooden spoon with a bunch of rubber bristles at the end of it. The food sticks to the bristles and the baby slurps the food off. You can also try using a clean finger and putting a small amount of baby food on the end of it.

Pick up Foods

Some babies are ready for pick up food in the beginning—at 6 months. Others do better at between 7 and 9 months of age. Finger foods can be small pieces of cheese, oat cereal or small cut up vegetables or meat. If your baby prefers feeding herself, let the baby do this and skip spoon-feeding altogether. Some babies will be poor feeders if left just to spoon feed but will improve their feeding habits when allowed to feed themselves.

Baby Led Weaning

This is an alternative approach to feeding a baby that skips the pureed stage and lets baby feed herself. Baby led feeding introduces baby to table foods right away.

Your baby should be approximately 6 months of age in order to use the baby led weaning method. The baby should be able to sit up without help and should have lost the tongue thrust reflex. The baby should be able to grasp foods and bring them up to her mouth.

Baby led meaning skips pureed food and offers your baby age appropriate soft-cooked or cut/mashed foods that are in easy to pick up pieces. You can even offer your baby a piece of apple to gnaw on or pieces of mashed fruit you cook yourself. The foods are just given to the baby to eat without using a spoon at all until your baby is ready to use the spoon independently.

You can cook the same vegetables your family is eating and mash a couple of table-spoonfuls of the vegetable for baby to eat on demand. In some ways, it's more of a hands-off approach than the spoon feeding method and it's a method that lets baby decide what she wants to eat and how much of it she wants to eat.

In baby led weaning, you don't simply fill up the baby's tray and walk away. You can sit by the child and encourage her eating certain foods. Or you can pull the highchair up to the table when the family eats and let the baby eat right along with the family and often with the same foods. You can encourage your baby and even guide food up to the mouth but don't put it in the mouth. The portion sizes are set by the baby and the baby will be gumming or chewing the food all on her own.

Most babies will eat exactly the right amount of the various foods you give her, especially if you take the time to put a variety of foods out there for baby. Advocates of baby led weaning believe that babies allowed to make their own choices early are able to better control what their bodies will need in the future and will make nourishing choices.

Will My Baby Get the Right Nutrients?

As long as you put food of a variety out there, the baby will naturally eat the right amounts of the right kinds of food. Pay attention to cues your baby will give out and put out those kinds of food the next time. Stop putting out food your baby isn't eating and try again in a week or two. Don't try and force feed the baby foods she doesn't want.

While you can start pureed foods at 4-6 months, it isn't a good idea to start table foods as you do in the baby led weaning program. You need to wait until it is an appropriate time to start foods that won't become a choking hazard. Each baby is different and will enjoy textures at her own pace. Just don't force it and remember that the baby is getting nutrition through breast milk or formula, too.

Only you can make the decision as to whether baby led weaning is appropriate for you and your baby. Try to strike up a conversation with your pediatrician to see how he or she feels about starting your baby on small pieces of table food rather than pureed food.

Chapter 4: Food Allergies

Like adults, babies can have allergies to certain foods. Interestingly, some of the allergies will pass when they get older and we'll talk about that later in this chapter. It's because of allergies that parents should wait 3-4 days before introducing a new food, especially if your family has a food allergy history. If you introduce foods one at a time when the baby is weaning to solids, you can gather a nice collection of foods your baby tolerates as well as those he doesn't tolerate.

By doing the four day rule, you are also doing what allergists call an "elimination diet". After the four days are up and you stop the food, you watch to see if the symptoms go away. By eliminating that food and getting relief of symptoms, you know that the food was the culprit all along.

If you don't follow the 3-4 day rule because you don't have allergies in your family, that's okay, too, but you could run into trouble with an allergy that you can't identify because your baby has taken in too many foods in too short a time. In fact, some pediatricians aren't recommending that parents wait 3-4 days at all because of studies showing that introducing allergenic food may not affect future allergies and the baby will outgrow the allergy anyway. If you have a personal or family history of food allergies, however, you may want to err on the side of caution.

Feed the baby new foods in the morning or at lunchtime. This will help you cope with whatever reaction you get and your pediatrician's office will be open for serious issues. You will disrupt your baby's nighttime schedule the least by feeding them new foods early in the day.

Symptoms of a Food Allergy

There are a lot of food allergy symptoms out there but these are the most common reactions you'll see:

- Sudden rashes, especially on the baby's bottom (but they can be anywhere)

- Loose stools with diarrhea and vomiting

- Hives

- Runny nose

- Gassiness or irritability after a meal

- Breathing problems after introducing a new food

- Swelling of the lips, tongue or face

- Tightening or closure of the throat

Don't forget that an allergy to food is different from intolerance to food. An intolerance to food yields intestinal problems such as diarrhea and gassiness only and doesn't yield rashes or other allergic symptoms.

Recent Changes to Recommendations

Increasingly, research studies in the last few years have recommended introducing allergenic foods to babies who are younger than 12 months. The studies claim that introducing allergenic foods around 4-6 months of age might actually provide protection against atopic (allergic) skin disease or asthma when the child is older. The studies indicate that it is okay to feed your child whole eggs at 6-7 months of age as opposed to just giving them egg yolks. It's only necessary to delay foods that you know are allergic to other members of your family.

In 2008, the American Academy of Pediatrics delivered a Policy Statement that said that solid foods should not be given before 4-6 months of age but, after that, there is no convincing evidence to indicate that delaying the introduction of foods beyond this period has a protective effect against the development of atopic diseases, even if foods are fed cow's milk versus breast milk. This includes the unnecessary delaying of foods like fish, eggs and peanut proteins.

Other studies included a German study showing that there was no evidence that a delayed introduction of solids past 4-6 months prevented allergic rhinitis, asthma or reactions to foods that are inhaled by the time the child reaches 6 years. Still another study showed that delaying the introduction of dairy products past 9 months is associated with an increased risk of asthma.

According to the ESPGHAN Report, exclusive breast feeding should be done until age 6 months with solids not introduced until 17 weeks and not later than 26 weeks. Delaying allergenic foods such as eggs and fish does not reduce allergies in babies or later in a child's life.

A Finnish study also looked into introducing solids late and found that it increased allergic sensitization to foods and to inhalant allergens. They found that wheat, eggs and oats were related to food sensitization and potatoes and fish products were related to inhalant sensitization or asthma.

An Australian study from 2010 found that infants who weren't given eggs until after 12 months of age were five times more likely to develop allergies compared to those who were introduced to eggs at four to six months.

Is My Baby Allergic or Intolerant to Foods?

Remember that an allergic reaction happens when the body is mistaken and believes something is harmful to the body when it really isn't. The body makes antibodies against the food and it creates an allergic reaction when bound to the food particle. IgE is the antibody used to create an allergic reaction. As part of its function, it causes the release of histamines, which causes hives.

Histamines also cause nasal drainage, itchy eyes, and sometimes anaphylaxis or a serious reaction that affects the throat and airways.

Food intolerance does not involve the immune system and involves other chemical reactions in the body. One example of this is citrus fruits which are very acidic and can irritate the gastrointestinal system. They can cause a problem some times and not at other times. Sometimes infants will break out in a rash around their mouth if given citrus fruits prior to a year of age. They can also have cramps in their stomach if given acidic citrus fruits too early.

Lactose intolerance is another type of food intolerance. When a baby is lactose intolerant, he lacks the proper enzyme to digest lactose in dairy products. Babies who are lactose intolerant can often eat cheese and yogurt because these products have been cultured enough to have lactose already broken down by the time the food is eaten. Lactose intolerance is different from cow's milk allergy.

Common Food Allergies

These are the most common food allergies—those you should be the most cautious about if your baby is prone to food allergies—include:

- Eggs
- Milk
- Peanuts
- Tree nuts like cashews and walnuts
- Shellfish
- Fish
- Soy
- Wheat

It is possible for a child to outgrow a food allergy to soybeans, wheat, milk and eggs over time. Don't forget that a wheat allergy is different from wheat intolerance. Wheat or gluten intolerance can't be outgrown and must be managed for the rest of one's life.

Honey

Honey does not cause allergies. Nevertheless, you should not give your baby honey. Honey contains spores of the bacteria that can cause botulism which could be deadly for a baby. Don't start giving your baby honey until he is at least one year of age.

Read through this chapter a couple of times so you don't get confused about what to give a baby and what not to give a baby at the various ages. The bottom line is that most babies can eat what you're eating by a year of age unless there is a specific allergy.

Chapter 5: Making Organic Baby Food

Homemade organic baby food starts with healthy organic foods. Maybe you've decided to go full-on organic and have gone organic yourself. Maybe, though, you want something better for your baby and you've read that organic baby food is best for babies. Organic baby food provides for your baby the freshest possible foods free of pesticides, chemicals, and hormones.

Some parents go all organic and others use a mixture of organic and non-organic foods. What you choose to do depends on you and on the availability of organic foods in your local stores or garden. Organic foods are a bit more expensive than non-organic food but for your baby, it may be more than worth it.

Organic baby food is truly better for your baby than non-organic food. There are no pesticides or other chemicals in the food and they are the best foods for your baby's fragile systems. There won't be any pesticides to overload the liver and there won't be any hormones to interfere with your baby's hormonal system.

Let's look at some advantages of using organic baby food for your baby:

- A baby consumes more pesticides pound for pound than adults because they ingest more fruits and vegetables per their body weight than adults.

- Babies who eat organic foods aren't exposed to pesticides, which are harmful to tissues

- Foods containing "nitrates" don't have as much nitrates in them if they are certified organic. Because nitrates are naturally occurring, you can't get rid of them completely.

- Studies reveal that organic foods have a higher nutritional value than conventionally-grown foods.

- Organic foods are not genetically modified. They must meet certain standards that include not being genetically modified.

Organic foods, by definition are grown with no chemical fertilizers or synthetic pesticides, which are carcinogens. Some organic food farmers are allowed to use organic pesticides that are technically found in nature, such as sulfur, copper, nicotine and nitrogen. Unfortunately, there exist no research studies that tell us whether or not these natural pesticide foods are any safer than inorganic pesticide foods but common sense points out that eating a peach grown with nonorganic pesticides and fertilizers is less safe than eating one grown with natural pesticides and fertilizers.

The beginning of organic baby food is organic food. You basically purchase organically grown potatoes, green beans, peas, carrots, squash, apples, peaches, bananas, and pears. You cook these foods by steaming them or boiling them so that they are soft and mushy. Then you mash the food with a potato masher or with a food processor or blender. Add as much water as necessary to make the baby food as thick or as thin as your baby can tolerate. There's no need to add salt as babies do not crave it and you can use breast milk or formula to thin the baby food instead of water.

Organic baby foods can be hard to come by. Some jarred baby food is organic and they aren't much more expensive than regular baby food. Organic food can also be expensive and it can seem overwhelming to be making all your baby's baby food. In the next chapter, we'll talk about storing baby food and you'll find it easier to make and store food for later. That way you won't be making baby food every day. And if organic food is more expensive than regular food, your baby's health is worth it. There is no reason not to buy organic and make organic baby food in quantities that are easy to store for a later date. Your baby's health depends on you giving them food that will help them grow safely.

When thinking of the expense and time of feeding your baby, try to remember that you are going out of your way to make sure your baby has fresh foods and is developing healthy eating habits that will grow to last a long time. The food has been proven by research to be better and healthier for our bodies. Some studies have shown that there are more nutrients in food grown organically when compared to food grown conventionally. For example, organic milk has 60-80 percent more nutrients in the summer when compared to conventional milk and contains 50-60 percent more nutrients in the winter when compared to conventional milk. It has higher levels of vitamin E as well. Cheese is similarly blessed when it is organic. Organic vegetables have 20-40 percent more nutrients than conventionally-grown vegetables.

Even though you may pay more than 50 percent more for organic fruits, meats, and vegetables, you'll be joining a growing rank of people who are buying organic. It's one of the fastest growing segments of the grocery industry. People in general are trying to reduce their overall exposure to chemicals in their food.

What Do the Labels Mean?

- **100 percent organic**. If you see a product with this label it means that legally it cannot have any synthetic ingredients and must be grown under federal organic standards. It must also mean that it has been inspected by accredited inspectors.

- **Organic**. A product with this label means that at least 95 percent of its ingredients were organically produced.

- **Made with organic ingredients**. If you see a product labeled like this, at least 70 percent of its makeup is in organic ingredients. The rest of the ingredients must come from an approved list put out by the US Department of Agriculture.

- **All Natural or "Natural"**. This is not the same thing as organic. There is no specific definition for this type of labeling with the exception of meat and poultry products, which are natural when they don't contain artificial flavoring.

- **Free Range**. There are no real government standards for this sort of thing except to mean that the animal was not caged and was allowed to run free for an undetermined period per day.

When you buy organic poultry, eggs, meat, and dairy, you are guaranteed not to be eating a product that has been fed with non-organic feed and you'll avoid products that are made with antibiotics or hormones. Giving these meat and poultry products antibiotics has been linked to antibiotic resistance in humans.

In later chapters, we'll talk about storing organic baby food and will provide you with some great recipes that will send you on your way to making your baby the best food available.

Chapter 6: Storing Organic Baby Food

It's probably easiest to make a large quantity of baby food and storing it in ways that will keep you swimming in baby food for a long time to come. The method you choose must be sanitary, yet convenient. Options include freezing segments with ice cube trays, storing it in the refrigerator, using glass baby food jars or putting clumps of baby food on waxed paper and freezing it on baking sheets. We will discuss the pros and cons of each method.

Ice Cube Tray Method

In this method, you make a large batch of baby food and spoon the pureed food into ice cube trays. You want to clean out the trays thoroughly with soap and water and you want to dry them with a clean cloth. Spoon in the baby food and cover it with a plastic wrap. If you have a dishwasher, you can clean the food trays on the "sanitary setting". You can also boil the ice cube trays if they tolerate the heat.

The ice cube tray has many great advantages:

- Each ice cube slot is about an ounce so you can keep track with what your baby is eating.

- Ice cube trays are usually on hand so you won't have to buy anything special.

- There isn't a lot of waste with this quantity of food so you can use as little as one cube at a time if your baby doesn't eat much.

- You can make as many baby food trays at a time so that you don't have to spend as much time cooking.

When the pureed food has been frozen, simply pop them out of the tray and use a freezer bag to store them in the freezer. Take out as many frozen cubes as you need and feed them to baby after they've thawed out. Freezer bags are a good idea because they take up less freezer space when compared to keeping them in trays. Besides, you need your ice cube trays to make more baby food.

Make sure you label each freezer bag with the type of baby food you've put into it and the date the food was made. A lot of baby food looks alike so you don't want to have to guess what's in which bag. Plus you can keep track of how long the food has been frozen in the freezer.

Storing Baby Food in the Refrigerator

The most obvious problem with this is that you can't store food long in the refrigerator so it is neither safe nor very convenient for you and your baby. You can store refrigerated baby food no longer than 48 hours. Any longer than that and bacterial overgrowth will build up in the food and it could cause food poisoning in your baby. If you decide to store baby food in the refrigerator, always store it so that you can take individual, never been eaten out of, baby food out of the refrigerator. This reduces the amount of contamination that would be in baby food from saliva. Don't feed your baby from a container and store the container for later use.

Wax Paper Technique

This involves using waxed paper and a baking sheet, dropping clumps onto the sheet and freezing it. It needs a lot of freezer space until it's frozen and it doesn't come in uniform cubes like the ice cube tray method. You'd have to transfer your clumps to a baggie of some sort or a plastic freezer container.

Freezing Glass Jars

You should never freeze food in a glass container unless the container is labeled for freezing. The food can expand, bursting the glass jar and it can leave behind microscopic shards of glass that you don't want to get in your food or fingers later on. Plastic containers are a far better choice if you can find plastic containers in small enough sizes. They do make freezable jars in 4 ounce sizes from the BALL Company that you can use and a few other manufacturers make glass jars for freezing food as small as baby food. Remember, once the food is thawed out, you need to use the entire contents within 48 hours and have to divide the food so that you don't refrigerate that which has been eaten out of.

A Note on Refrigeration

Never assume that the refrigerator is of the right temperature. Your refrigerator should be kept at 40 degrees F at all times. If it runs higher than that, it can cause dangerous bacteria to grow and contaminate the food. Check the running temp of your thermometer using a refrigerator thermometer. An appliance thermometer would work also. Place the thermometer in water on the middle shelf and wait 6-8 hours to get a good reading of what your refrigerator temperature is running. Keep the refrigerator free of dust and leftover food particles as this can affect the running temperature.

A Note on Freezing

When you freeze foods, you should keep the freezer running at 0 degrees F and never above 5 degrees F. You should keep your freezer filled in order to have it running as smoothly as possible and use a freezer thermometer to check how it's doing every once in a while. The coldest part of the refrigerator in upright models is the tip shelf. Chest freezers tend to be coldest at the bottom. Put your baby food in these areas.

Storing Baby Food after a Power Outage

Much of your decision as to what to do after a power outage depends on how long the outage was and on what you did with the food when the outage was happening. If you expect a power outage, transfer refrigerated food to the freezer. Freeze containers of water around the food so it stays as cold as possible. If you have ice packs or gel packs, store baby food inside gel pack wraps inside a cooler. Avoid opening the refrigerator or freezer during an outage unless you really need something inside them. A freezer kept closed should maintain a good temperature if it is full for 48 hours. If it is only half full, it will hold the proper temperature for only 24 hours.

If you are freezing breast milk and the power is out for a long period of time, ask the firemen at your local fire department if they would store it for you in their freezers. They have generators that can keep the electricity running. After the outage is over with, use an appliance thermometer to see if the refrigerator is below 40 degrees F. If it isn't, throw the baby food away. If frozen food still contains crystals of ice in it, cook it up or refreeze it. The FDA states that outages less than 4 hours are probably okay but if the food was stored at 40 degrees or above for 2 hours or longer, you should throw away fish, meat, leftovers, eggs and baby food. Even if they are cooked through later, disease can still happen if you try to cook it after it has spoiled.

The Penny Trick

If you're going on a trip and you want to make sure there wasn't a power outage in your absence, put a penny on top of an ice cube in your freezer. If the outage was long enough to melt part of the ice cube, the penny will sink to the bottom of the ice cup tray. Even if everything is now frozen, if the penny was on the bottom of the ice cube, it was once unacceptably thawed out.

Microwaving Baby Food

Can you microwave baby food? Yes, you can microwave baby food if you are really careful about not overheating the food. Baby food can become severely hot and cause burns if you aren't an expert in microwaving food. The stove top is infinitely safer. Another good technique is placing baby food in a jar and putting the jar in a bowl of hot water. Leave it in the bowl for several minutes and it will warm to room temperature or more but not too hot.

If you do use the microwave, heat it for just a few seconds and let it sit a few minutes before testing and feeding to the baby. The baby really doesn't mind room temperature food and it isn't bad to feed a baby food that is room temperature.

Chapter 7: Weaning from Bottle or Breast to Cup

Babies love their bottles—so much that to switch to a cup can be traumatic and difficult to do. Bottles have meant security their whole life—or at least part of it if they were breastfed for a period of time. Even so, pediatricians recommend that parents begin to wean their child from bottle to cup by the time they are one year of age.

The two main reasons why you should wean the baby from the bottle at twelve months are:

- **Drinking from the bottle too long can damage baby's teeth.** Toddlers tend to drink while walking around and drink for prolonged periods of time. If the bottle contains anything other than water, it contains an acidic solution that can ultimately cause dental caries. Juice is particularly a bad choice for baby bottles.

- **Bottle drinkers drink more liquid than cup-fed babies.** They can drink up to 32 ounces a day, when toddlers need to take in only about 16 to 24 ounces per day. Babies drink milk instead of eating solid foods so they're missing out on the nutrient they'd get from solid foods.

By the time the baby is 12 months old, they have the motor skills to hold a cup, sit up and to drink from the cup. They no longer need the bottle. One year olds are less stubborn and have shorter memory spans so that they will be easier to wean. If you miss that window of opportunity, your toddler could be strongly attached to the bottle and your task of weaning the baby from the bottle will be tougher. Even if you've missed the window of opportunity, you have some options that will be explained later.

Before Switching

Start by the time the baby is between 9 and 12 months old. They're often quite ready to make the switch from bottle to cup. Phasing out the bottle requires a little bit of planning, however.

- You need to start at six months, letting the baby drink from a sippy cup. This acquaints the baby with the sippy cup when it is really time to make the change.

- Try putting the baby in the bathwater with the cup. They can play with it or drink with it, making as big a mess as they can.

- Don't offer only juice in a cup and milk in a bottle. This might make your baby refuse to drink milk out of a cup and will only take it with a bottle.

- If you breastfed exclusively through 9-12 months, you can skip using the bottle altogether and will go from breastfeeding to drinking from a cup.

Phasing out Gradually

This is a more moderate approach that works well with younger toddlers. Over a period of about one month you decrease the number of bottles you off, one at a time, and replace them with cups of milks or snacks. Water down the milk in the bottle but provide undiluted milk when given in a cup. Phase out the least important ones first, which usually are the bottles given in the middle of the day.

Try being creative, such as letting the child pick up a new cup or decorate one you already have. Try using a silly straw because it makes the cups more appealing. If you wean your 12-15 month old gradually, he or she will not miss the morning or evening bottle by the time you're done

Going Cold Turkey

For a baby that's strongly attached to the bottle, a gradual disappearance of the bottles might be too agonizing for the baby. A sudden withdrawal of the bottle might be really painful but still may be the most effective way to wean the baby off the bottle. Remind the baby what a big girl or boy he is so that he or she doesn't need the bottles anymore. Then you need to physically remove the bottles from the house.

Older toddlers respond to the idea that new babies need bottles now so he can wrap up his bottles like a present to give to the new babies out there. Then just put them in them in the mailbox and take them out later to the trash. This allows your toddler a chance to participate in the decision to get rid of bottles for an altruistic reason.

Give your toddler some kind of reward or snack for not drinking out of a bottle the whole day. This reinforces good behavior and gives the toddler a sense of accomplishment. Have a cup of water or juice available for times he or she wants the bottle the most. Talk to your child about replacing the bottle with a soothing transitional object like a teddy bear. He can hug the teddy bear whenever he gets lonely for the bottle. There may be trial and error when doing this kind of weaning but, once you're successful at a plan that works, you'll get good results.

Some parents delay weaning because they think it will be so difficult or time-consuming. Babies, too, are messy with food and drink and this can turn off a family when it comes time for weaning. But babies really do catch on to the hand eye coordination it takes to sip from a cup and keep the cup upright when they're done. You only have to endure a few days or weeks of instability. The earlier you start with sipping from a cup, the better it will be when you decide to go all the way and wean completely to a cup. Sipping from a cup is a learning experience. They don't have to have perfect hand eye coordination to begin the process.

Breastfed babies might be showing an inclination toward being weaned if they suck on the breast a few times and then quit or decide not to breastfeed altogether. The baby can become easily distracted while breastfeeding. She can show an interest in drinking from a cup as a sign it's ready to stop breastfeeding and use a cup.

Weaning the Parents

Weaning is tough on parents, too. This is a transition from babyhood toddlerhood and not many parents are willing to give up their baby. You're not ready to say that sad, long goodbye to infancy. Acknowledge this and know that, however painful weaning is, the rewards will be great and your baby will have gone through a very necessary transition. Bond with your baby through cuddling or reading a book rather than breastfeeding or bottle feeding in your arms.

Tips and Tricks to Weaning

Try these tips for successful weaning. It really doesn't have to be an ordeal:

1. Don't wean when your lives are already stressful. If you're moving or starting a new job, it's better to wait until you are settled.

2. If the baby is sick, breast or bottle feed them for comfort. It may help your baby begin to feel better sooner if he's exposed to something he likes.

3. Always follow the child's lead. If they appear ready, then use that as your guide. If they're not ready, their behavior will show it.

4. Give other sources of calcium in the diet, such as cheese or yogurt, especially if he isn't taking in a full 16 ounces of baby formula per day while weaning.

5. Make sure that baby is beginning to eat solid foods by 6 months old, even if he isn't weaned. This means that breast milk or formula milk won't be the sole source of nutrition at one year of age or weaning time.

6. Put formula or breast milk in the weaning cup. This will increase the chance that the baby will take what's offered in the sippy cup.

7. Babies are getting liquid in the pureed food they eat, too. This means that their actual liquid content in sippy cups or bottles is naturally going to be lower than before.

8. If you're breastfeeding, try to be patient. It takes about 2-4 weeks to completely dry up after stopping breastfeeding.

9. Remember that weaning can be gradual or all at once. It really depends on your comfort level and on your baby's comfort level.

Chapter 8: Graduating to Toddler Food

At some point, your baby will have teeth and the ability to chew. She will have the manual dexterity to pick up small pieces of food and put them in her mouth. She will become bored with being fed pureed food all the time and will want to master the spoon herself. Your baby's tummy won't be as sensitive and her diet will more closely resemble your own. In this chapter, we'll look at what a toddler's diet should look like and how to make it as varied as possible.

What is a Toddler?

Loosely speaking, a toddler is a child between the ages of 12 months and 48 months who loves to eat one food one day and then refuses to eat the very same food the next day.

He or she often requires a lot of cleaning up after, laundry, attention, constant amusement and stimulation. He or she will be nourishing both body and mind during these years and parents have to keep track of both. A toddler is a child whose innocence and wonder inspires us all and helps us to do better will all the love and patience we have. He or she is an unconditional giver and lover, giving love to all who will receive and who has hugs and kisses for pets and humans alike. A toddler is a true blessing and joy to be able to treasure.

What Toddlers Eat

There is a plethora of "toddler food out there" from toddler yogurt to toddler gummy bears to pick-up pieces of carrots but you really don't have to get that fancy. Toddler crackers are not really different than adult crackers and you can make carrots and cut them up with no difference in nutrition. When thinking of "what to feed the toddler", think about the food groups and what you yourself think of eating. Let's take a look:

- **Protein**: This includes meats and eggs, primarily. We'll discuss milk protein in the next section. Toddlers can eat scrambled eggs or crumbled poached eggs that are of the size to pick up and eat. Eggs contain a natural source of vitamin D which helps your toddler absorb calcium for strong bones and teeth. They can also eat meat, such as cut-up pieces of meat loaf, pieces of chicken cut up, ham slices that are cut up and turkey pieces cut up. Stick to the lean meats so your toddler doesn't get used to eating fatty meats.

- **Milk Protein**: After one year of age, your baby gives up formula and sticks with whole milk. Whole milk is recommended because, up to age two, pediatricians recommend that your baby get the milk solids and milk fat in whole milk. Speaking of milk solids, there is always yogurt to eat, which contains fruit for a great tasting meal and cottage cheese. If you use large curd cottage cheese, the pieces are able to be picked up easily by the toddler. With small curd cottage cheese, he might have to use a spoon or toddler fork.

- **Fruit**: Fruits can be just about anything because they all contain essential vitamins and minerals. Whole fruits contain fiber to keep bowel movements regular. Fruit can be pieces of melon cut up in small parts, berries, kiwifruit, orange slices and cut up pears or peaches. The little cups of mixed fruit, tangerine slices or applesauce are perfect foods for a breakfast, lunch or dinner. The quantities in these cups are just about enough for one serving.

- **Vegetables**: Get your toddler used to vegetables early and often. Vegetables can be peas, cut up carrots, eggplant, zucchini, summer squash, corn, asparagus, green beans or just about any other vegetable grown in the garden or purchased from the store.

- **Grains**: Grains are a wide category of food from oatmeal to bread. Kids can eat oatmeal in the morning because studies show it helps them concentrate better when in school. Cream of Rice is a good choice if the child can handle a spoon and, for those that don't handle a spoon well, they can try crackers, especially whole grain crackers, and pieces of bread and butter. Try to stick to whole grains so your child doesn't grow up to be a white bread adult. Don't forget whole grain pasta, which comes in many sizes and shapes.

The Best Finger Foods

Toddlers love finger foods. Eating them gives a toddler a sense of independence and choice. Eating them also provides good nutrition disguised as snacks. Here are top 10 finger foods for toddlers.

1. **Sweet Potatoes**. They come as sweet potato fries which are high in vitamins A and C, or microwaved whole and cut up. It takes about 2-5 minutes to bake a whole sweet potato. Kids love them because they are a little bit sweet.

2. **Frozen Peas**. These have loads of fiber in them and are rich in vitamins and minerals. You can cook them in the microwave or on the stove. You can also let them thaw out on their own and provide them as a snack for your toddler.

3. **Soft Meat**. Well cooked chicken or pieces of lunch meat or pork are soft enough for toddlers to chew and they are less likely to choke on them. Fifteen percent of toddlers under three aren't getting enough iron in their diet. Soft meats can give them a good source of iron.

4. **Fish**. This can include well-made fish sticks or baked sole, which are high in DHA and EPA, which are healthy fatty acids. Toddlers, just like adults, can't make these essential fatty acids so they need to get it in their diet. Canned light tuna can be picked up as can grilled tilapia, cut up in small pieces. Look for fish sticks that are made with salmon as they are healthier than regular fish sticks.

5. **Eggs**. Eggs are high in quality protein and have vitamin B12, riboflavin, iron and choline for good health. They can be scrambled with vegetables or boiled and cut up for finger food.

6. **Soft Fruits and Vegetables**. Cut up fruits and vegetables make great snacks and teach your child to like these excellent sources of vitamins and minerals. Vitamin

C fruits are a great choice as well as vitamin A containing steamed vegetables.

7. **Grated Apple**. Just peel the skin off the apple and grate the apple. It will be soft enough and easy to pick up. It has a high fiber content and is great for your toddler's immune system.

8. **Grated Cheese**. Put a clump of grated cheese on your toddler's high chair and let them pick it up to munch on. Cheese has tons of protein and calcium in it and it has the fat in it that toddlers up to the age of two really need.

9. **Beans**. Great sources of vitamin B, iron and fiber, these protein-rich little beans make the perfect pick up food for toddlers. Cook them so they are really soft and serve them with guacamole or just cut up avocadoes.

10. **Whole Grains**. This usually means noodles of any kind or shape. They make whole grain noodles which are especially good with or without some kind of sauce.

Chapter 9: Organic Baby Food Recipes

Now that you know how to get your baby to take in solids and know which things are good for her, you can begin to collect recipes of baby food that will give your baby some variety in what she eats. Recipes include a variety of fruits, vegetables, meats and grains that will help your baby get the nutritional variety they might not get if you don't choose your baby's food well. While we won't say it in every recipe, we're expecting you to use organic vegetables, fruits and meats to make this baby food as it provides better nutrition for baby. Here is a selection of baby food recipes that will be a good start for your recipe collection:

Banana Oatmeal with Blueberries

This is a great source of fiber, vitamin C, vitamin A and antioxidants for your baby.

Ingredients:

- 1/4 c plain oatmeal (not instant)
- 1 tablespoon organic blueberries
- 1 tablespoon whole milk yogurt
- 1/2 small banana, ripe

Directions:

Cook oats with water until cooked. Add yogurt to cooked oats and put the whole thing in a blender. Add bananas and blueberries to mixture and blend until smooth.

Potatoes and Pumpkin with Apple Snack

Ingredients:

- 1-2 apples
- 1/4 of one small pumpkin
- 1 potato, small

Directions:

Peel all vegetables and fruits and cut them up. Cook in water over low heat until soft, about 20 minutes. Blend in blender until smooth and serve at the proper temperature.

Pureed Pudding with Brown Rice

The brown rice will give your baby the fiber he or she needs for healthy bowel movements.

Ingredients:

- 1 c cooked brown rice
- 1/4 c raisins
- Pinch of nutmeg
- 2/3 c formula or breast milk
- Pinch of cinnamon

Directions:

Simmer raisins in apple juice for 10 minutes and then add the rest of the ingredients, bringing them to a boil. Stir as it cooks and lower to simmering again. Cover and simmer for about ten minutes. Mixture will be thick. Then puree in blender or food processor until pureed.

Chicken with Lentils

This is a meal appropriate for babies seven months of age or older.

Ingredients:

- 1 small zucchini, diced and peeled
- 1/4 c sweet potato, diced and peeled
- 1 tablespoon red lentils
- 1/4 c chopped chicken breast, skin removed
- 1/4 c cauliflower, chopped up
- 3/4 c breast milk or formula

Directions:

Make sure lentils have no stones and rinse with cold water. Put all ingredients in pan and boil. Then lessen the heat to simmering and simmer for 25 minutes until vegetables are sauce and chicken is cooked through. Add more milk if it is too thick. Then puree until it is smooth.

Creamy Apricots

This mixes fruit and dairy for a tasty treat!

Ingredients:

- 1/2 c apple juice
- 1/2 c organic dried apricots
- 1/2 c plain whole milk yogurt

Directions:

Boil the dried apricots and apple juice together. Lower heat and simmer the mixture for ten minutes. Puree the mixture in a blender or food processor and then mix the pureed fruit into the yogurt. Serve chilled.

Lamb with Vegetables

This is a meal for babies who are 7 months old or older. It is high in protein and vitamins.

Ingredients:

- 1 potato, cubed and peeled
- 1 c formula or breast milk
- 1 zucchini, peeled and cubed
- 1 carrot, cubed and peeled
- 1 small shank of lamb
- 1 teaspoon fresh mint, chopped

Directions:

Brown the lamb in oil and cover with water. Bring the lamb to a boil and lower heat to simmer. Simmer until lamb is soft and cooked through. Simmer veggies in milk until tender. Cut lamb into small pieces after removing bone. Mix lamb with veggies and milk. Add chopped mint and puree until mixed and smooth.

Carrot and Parsnip Puree

Ingredients:

- 1 carrot, medium
- 1 parsnip, medium
- Small pinch of nutmeg

Directions:

Peel veggies and dice them. Simmer in water until tender. Drain the veggies but reserve the water. Puree with nutmeg, adding back water until thickness is appropriate.

Butternut Squash with Pears

Ingredients:

- 1 butternut squash
- 1 pear, ripe

Directions:

Peel squash and cut in half. Take out seeds and cut squash in cubes. Peel and core pear and cut in cubes. Steam the butternut squash for fifteen minutes and add pears for an additional 5-8 minutes of steaming. When all is soft and tender, puree the mixture adding breast milk or formula if it is too thick.

Puree of Plantains and Sweet Potatoes

Ingredients:

- 1 plantain, peeled and chopped
- 1/4 c breast milk or formula
- 1 c sweet potato, cooked and mashed
- 3/4 c chicken stock, low sodium
- 1/4 c plain organic yogurt
- 1 teaspoon of fresh, chopped parsley
- Pinch of pepper

Directions:

Boil plantain in chicken broth and then simmer for 10 minutes until plantain is soft. Drain this mixture, saving the cooking liquid. Mix all ingredients in food processor or blender adding extra water if it's too thick. Warm the puree to proper temperature.

Creamy Tofu and Avocado

This recipe is designed for those 8 months old or older.

Ingredients:

- 1/2 c silken tofu
- 1 diced avocado
- 1/2 c fresh chives, chopped

Directions:

Mash the tofu with avocado and mix in chives. Chill this and serve.

Pureed Bananas

This is perfect for 4-6 months of age. This recipe is rich in vitamin C, vitamin A, folate, and minerals.

Ingredients:

- 1 banana, uncooked and ripe

Directions:

Peel the banana if it's ripe and put it in a blender or food processor to puree. Bananas can also be mashed with a fork. Cook in microwave for 25 seconds to further soften the bananas. Add water, formula or breast milk to thin it. Add cereal if it needs thickening.

Mango Delight

This is appropriate for 6-8 month old babies and is rich in vitamins A, C, E, K and folate as well as the minerals, potassium, phosphorus, magnesium, calcium and sodium.

Ingredients:

- Formula, Breast milk or Water
- 1 mango, ripe

Directions:

Peel and cut the mango in half. Remove seeds and make chunks out of the mango. Puree the mango in the food processor or blender, adding liquid ingredient of choice to make the puree the right consistency.

Papaya Puree

This is for babies at least 6-8 months of age. Papaya can be eaten raw if it is ripe. It contains vitamins A, C, and Folate, along with the minerals Calcium and Potassium.

Ingredients:

- 1 ripe papaya
- Water, formula or breast milk

Directions:

Peel papaya and remove seeds. Put papaya into chunks and puree it. Thin the puree with water, formula or breast milk. Add cereal if it gets too thin. If you feel the baby won't tolerate the raw fruit, steam it gently after chunking it for about 5-10 minutes.

Fruit Puree

This involves using any combination of pears, plums, nectarines and peaches to make a fruit puree. Pears are okay from 4-6 months or more but you need to steam it gently if the baby is under the age of 6 months. Pears should be pureed and watered down with formula or breast milk and can be thickened with rice cereal.

Plums are for 6-8 months of age or older and contains vitamins C, folate and A with minerals Phosphorus, Potassium, Calcium and Magnesium. Peel two to three ripe plums and remove pits. Chunk the fruit and steam until tender in a bit of water if the baby is under 6 months. Puree the fruit and use breast milk or baby formula if it's too thick and add rice cereal if it is too thin for your baby. Mix in another fruit with plums because they tend to be too bitter or tart alone.

Peaches contain A, Folate and C vitamins along with Calcium, Magnesium, Phosphorus or Potassium. Start by baking or steaming peaches. Peel the peach and cook it. Baked peaches are especially good. Cut into chunks and puree using formula or breast milk to thin or rice cereal to thicken. This is good for babies 6-8 months of age or older.

Baked Peaches

Ingredients:

- 1 peach
- Water

Directions:

Cut fruit in half and remove seed. Place cut side down in a pan that contains 1 inch of water. Bake at 400 degrees F until the skin puckers. Remove skin and save extra water to thin out the puree.

Pumpkin Puree

This is a good recipe for 6-8 months old infants or more. It contains Vitamin A, Vitamin K, Vitamin C, folate and niacin, along with the minerals iron, calcium, magnesium, phosphorus, and potassium.

Ingredients:

- One small sugar pumpkin, less than 5 pounds

Directions:

Cut pumpkin in half and remove seeds. Place halves face down in an inch of water on a baking sheet. Keep water level up and bake at 400 degrees F for 40 minutes. Scoop out the meat of the pumpkin and puree it in a blender or food processor. Add water to achieve the right consistency for your baby. Incidentally, you might also boil chunks of pumpkin in water and remove the skin after the meat is tender.

Green Beans

These are perfect for 4-6 months of age an contains vitamins A. C, K, Niacin, Folate and the minerals Potassium, Sodium, Phosphorus, Magnesium, Iron and Calcium. Peas can be made with this recipe, too.

Ingredients:

- Fresh green beans

Directions:

Snap the ends off the green beans and snap into pieces. If using peas, scrape peas out of pots. Steam in a small amount of water until tender. Keep checking on the water level. Keep left over water in case the beans/peas need to be thinned. Puree with blender or food processor and thin with steam water until the right consistency for your baby. Push through a strainer to get any skins to be removed.

Carrots

These are great sources for vitamin A, C and folate. It contains the minerals potassium, sodium, iron, magnesium, phosphorus and calcium.

Ingredients:

- Fresh carrots

Directions:

Peel and cut up carrots. Steam carrots until they are tender. Don't use leftover carrot steaming water if the baby is less than eight months old because nitrates can leach into the water. Puree using a blender or food processor. Add back water as needed to make the carrots the right consistency for your baby.

Garden Veggie Combo

This is a great veggie combo for babies 6-8 months of age. Mix and match vegetables as you have access to them. Use peas, carrots, summer squash and green beans.

Directions:

Mix the various vegetables as you have availability of them. Add enough water to cover vegetables and boil until tender, saving water for later. Puree all vegetables together in a food processor or blender. Add water back for the desired consistency.

Squash

Use winter squash, butternut squash, acorn squash and Hubbard squash for kids age six months or older.

Directions:

Cut squash in half and scoop out the seeds. Put them cut side down in an inch of water on a baking sheet. Keep checking on the water level. Cook at 400 degrees F for 40 minutes or until the shell puckers. Scoop out the meat from the shell and puree in a blender or food processor. Add water to create the desired consistency. Squash can be chunked and boiled, removing the skin after the meat gets tender.

Zucchini or Summer Squash

This is good for at least 6-8 months.

Directions:

Select the squash or zucchini that is narrow in diameter because they are the most tender. Wash the squash or zucchini and peel with a potato peeler. Cut the squash into chunks. Steam until squash is tender and puree with a blender or food processor. Add back water to create the consistency you were looking for.

Sweet Potatoes or Yams

This contains a great deal of vitamin A, vitamin C and folate along with the minerals sodium, phosphorus, selenium, calcium and magnesium.

Directions:

Wash sweet potatoes and poke holes in it, wrapping it in tin foil or wrapping in plastic wrap in the microwave. Cook in microwave for 8 minutes or until tender. Cook in oven for 30 minutes at 400 degrees. Remove skins from sweet potato and just use the flesh. Puree in blender or food processor and add water back to desired consistency.

Fish, Sweet Potato and Broccoli Puree

Babies can handle fish, especially when mixed with vegetables. This was designed for babies at least 6 months of age.

Ingredients:

- 2 broccoli florets, cut in small pieces
- 1/2 of a sweet potato, diced
- 1/4 c milk
- 4 oz fillet of sole
- 2 tbsp shredded cheese

Directions:

Steam broccoli and sweet potato for about 6-8 minutes. Cover fish in a saucepan and cover with milk. Cook until it easily flakes, at least 2 minutes. Stir in cheese until it gets melted. Puree the entire mixture in a food processor or blender. Add milk to make the consistency right. Cool quickly on ice and re-frigerate. You can also freeze individual portions in the freezer. Heat in skillet or in the microwave until warm for baby's palate.

Apple and Oat Puree

Select a sweet apple to make sure your applesauce is naturally sweet. Homemade applesauce contains plenty of fiber for baby's bowels. Oats have vitamins, minerals and essential fatty acids. They also stabilize your baby's blood sugar. This recipe is for babies 6 months old or more.

Ingredients:

- 1 tablespoon baby oatmeal
- 3 sweet apples, thinly sliced, peeled and cored
- 1 teaspoon agave nectar
- 2 tablespoons of water
- Pinch of cinnamon
- 3 tablespoons breast milk or formula

Directions:

Put apple slices in 2 tbsp water. Boil and then simmer for 10-15 minutes. Add cinnamon and puree in a blender or food processor. Add agave nectar (optional) for sweetness. Cool applesauce until needed. Take out 2 tbsp applesauce and stir in oatmeal and milk. Cool to the right temperature for baby and serve.

Corn Chowder with Chicken

Chicken is a great starter meat for babies. It is tender and mild in flavor. You can make it this way with corn chowder or in another recipe, mixed with apples and sweet potatoes. This is a good recipe for babies 6-9 months of age.

Ingredients:

- 1 potato, diced, peeled
- 1 chicken breast, boneless and without skin, cubed
- 1 1/2 c corn packed in water, organic. Drain out 1/3 cup water and drain the rest of the corn.
- 1-2 tablespoons breast milk or formula

Directions:

Put corn, 1/3 cup water and chicken into a heatproof bowl inside saucepan. Put potato in saucepan and pour boiling water over the potato so the water reaches halfway up bowl. Boil water and then simmer for about ten minutes or until chicken is cooked through. Remove bowl from pan and drain potato of water. Puree potato or put in a baby food mill. Add chicken and corn mixture plus cooking liquid from bowl and puree the whole thing. Press through sieve to get rid of corn skins so the consistency is smoother. Cool and refrigerate or freeze your individual baby portions.

Squash and Sweet Potato Puree

The naturally sweet flavors of squash and sweet potato lend themselves to the baby's palate. These foods are high in beta-carotene, a form of vitamin A. Use this recipe on 6-9 month old babies.

Ingredients:

- 2 tablespoons olive oil
- 1 small butternut squash, cut in cubes, peeled and seeded
- 2 tablespoons water
- 1 sweet potato, cut in 1 inch cubes, peeled
- Breast milk or formula to achieve consistency

Directions:

Set oven to 400 degrees F. Put foil to cover a baking sheet and spread sweet potato and butternut squash onto sheet. Drizzle water and olive oil over veggies. Cover with another piece of foil and seal at edges. Bake for 30 minutes or until vegetables soft. Cool veggies and put in food processor or blender. Thin with milk to achieve consistency. If you're go-

ing to freeze meals, add milk after thawing
out the meal. Serve slightly warm.

Puree of Squash, Beef and Tomatoes

Mixing vegetables with beef help fussy babies tolerate the beefy taste better.

Ingredients:

- 1/2 c ground round beef
- 2 plum tomatoes
- 1/4 small butternut squash, peeled, de-seeded and grated
- 1 teaspoon olive oil
- 2/3 c vegetable stock

Directions:

Cut a cross in the bottom of each tomato and put them in a heat tolerant bow covered with boiled water. Let stand for 30 seconds and place tomatoes in cold water to peel off the skins. Cut in quarters and remove seeds. Chop up the flesh. Heat olive oil in frying pan and sauté the beef until cooked and crumbled, about 2-3 minutes. Add squash and tomato, sautéing until vegetables are soft—about 2 minutes. Add the stock and bring to a boil, then simmering for ten minutes. Cool the mixture slightly and then puree the entire contents of the pan, adding extra water to achieve

the right consistency. Freeze in individual portions.

Apple, Peach and Pear Delight

This is a great meal when all these fruits are seasonally rip. You can also add plums or apricots. For extra sweetness, add agave nectar (1 tsp) if you wish. This is a good recipe for babies 6-9 months old.

Ingredients:

- 1 ripe pear (all peeled and cored or pit removed)
- 2 ripe peaches
- 1 sweet apple
- 2 tbsp water

Directions:

Cut a cross at the bottom and top of each peach and put them in a heat tolerant bowl. Run boiling water over it and let sit 30 seconds. Put in cold water immediately and allow the skin to peel off. Cut in fourths and remove pit. Then dice the entire peach. Dice apples and pear as well and put together in saucepan with water. Boil and then simmer on low, cooking for about ten minutes or until fruit is soft. Cool and then puree until smooth, adding water back if it's too thick. Freeze in individual portions and thaw for one to two hours before serving.

Potato, Cauliflower and Cheese Puree

This is a good baby food for hungry babies because it's very filling. You can use sweet potato instead of regular potato. It cooks three minutes faster than white potato. The recipe is great for babies aged 6-9 months.

Ingredients:

- 1 sweet potato or potato, peeled and cubed into small cubes
- 1 c shredded cheese
- 1/4 head cauliflower, chopped up
- 2-4 tablespoons formula or breast milk

Directions:

Steam potato cubes in a single layer for about 5 minutes, covered. Add cauliflower to the steamer and cover until vegetables are tender, about 8-10 minutes. Blend the vegetables until pureed and then add the cheese and breast milk or formula. Puree with extra milk to make for a nice texture and thickness. Freeze individual portions and reheat in microwave or on stove. Check temperature before serving.

Beef Casserole

Kids need iron by six months of age, which can be gotten from meat. Red meat is best for low iron. Cook it with veggies for a soft puree. You get plenty of iron, protein, potassium, selenium, beta-carotene, zinc and prebiotics from this meal, perfect for babies aged 6-9 months of age.

Ingredients:

- 1 small onion
- 2 potatoes, peeled and chopped
- 1 tablespoon olive oil
- 1 large sweet potato, peeled and chopped
- 1 clove garlic
- 2 tablespoon tomato paste
- 1/4 teaspoon of fresh thyme
- 4 oz lean chuck, cut in small chunks
- 1 cup chicken stock

Directions:

Heat oil in large pot and sauté onion for 5 minutes. Add thyme and garlic, cooking an additional minute. Sauté chuck steak for a few minutes until it is seared. Then add tomato paste, sautéing an additional minute. Add sweet potato, potatoes and chicken stock. Boil the mixture and then simmer for 50 minutes until everything is soft. Cool for a little and then puree, adding stock if it needs to be thinned.

Lentils with Tomatoes and Carrots

These foods are antioxidants and contain lycopene, another antioxidant. Use quick cooking lentils for great fiber, folate and iron. This is for babies 9-12 months of age.

Ingredients:

- 1 c coconut milk, canned
- 1 tablespoon olive oil
- 2/3 c red lentils
- 2 skinned tomatoes, seeds removed and chopped
- 1/4 teaspoon ground cumin
- 2 grated carrots
- 1/4 teaspoon ground coriander
- 1 1/4 c vegetable stock

Directions:

Sauté the tomatoes and carrots in oil until soft—about five minutes. Stir in spices and cook an additional thirty seconds. Add coconut milk, lentils and stock. Boil and then bring to a simmer until lentils are soft. This should take about 20 minutes. Puree the entire batch or mash with a masher for more texture.

Chicken Curry with Fruit

Because it is spicy, it is best for babies aged 12-18 months to tempt their palates to try more adventurous foods.

Ingredients:

- 1 teaspoon tomato paste
- 2 tablespoons sunflower oil
- 7 ounces butternut squash, chopped and peeled
- 1 chicken breast, cubed
- 1 small shallot, finely chopped
- 2 teaspoons mild Korma curry paste
- Dried apricots, two, chopped
- 2/3 c unsalted chicken stock

Directions:

Sauté shallot in oil for four minutes. Add chicken pieces and sauté until the outside is white. Stir in curry paste. Add rest of ingredients and simmer for ten minutes. Then puree the entire mixture.

Chicken Puree for Babies

Introduce your baby to chicken early. It is easily digested and made sweet by the addition of sweet potato and dried apricots. Chicken thigh is used in this recipe because it has more zinc and iron in it than white meat and is softer than white meat. This is for babies 6-9 months of age.

Ingredients:

- 2/3 c pureed tomatoes
- 2 thighs of chicken
- 1/3 c dried apricots cut in half
- 2 c peeled, chopped sweet potato
- 1 tablespoon of olive oil
- 1/2 cup leeks, sliced
- Nearly 1 cup of chicken or vegetable stock

Directions:

Take meat off chicken thighs and get rid of the fat, bones and skin. Cut meat into small chunks. Heat oil in saucepan and sauté the leeks until soft. Add chicken and sauté until all sides of meat chunks are white, about two minutes. Add sweet potato, sautéing for a minute. Add dried apricots, tomato puree and chicken stock. Boil everything first and then simmer for 15 minutes. Cool slightly and blend into a puree with a food processor or blender.

Salmon Dinner with Potatoes and Carrots

Salmon is rich in essential fatty acids that help brain and eye development. If mashing potatoes make them too lumpy, use a baby food grinder or potato ricer to make the potatoes. This is the perfect recipe for ages 6-9 months. It has a large supply of omega-3 fatty acids, protein, iron, calcium, selenium, vitamin A, beta-carotene, and vitamin D.

Ingredients:

- 1/3 c shredded cheese
- 1 c sliced carrots, peeled
- 1 tablespoon butter
- 2 c chopped potatoes, peeled
- 3.5 tablespoons milk
- 4 ounces of salmon

Directions:

Cover potatoes and carrots with boiling water in saucepan and cook until vegetables soft, about 20 minutes. Mash together after draining. Include 3 tbsp milk, butter and cheese with the mashing of the vegetables. Put salmon into dish with 1/2 tbsp milk and microwave 1.5 minutes. Flake the fish so there are no bones. Mash fish into potato/carrot mixture.

Infant Pick Up Foods

By 7-8 months, many babies are in a position to pick up foods and put them in their mouths. The foods selected below can be described as pick up foods because babies have a hand in getting the food into their bodies, chewing and swallowing. Let's see what's out there:

Breakfast Fruit

Ingredients:

- 2 tablespoons yogurt, plain
- 1/2 small banana
- 2 tablespoons ground oatmeal or baby oatmeal
- 2 tablespoons ripe peach, peeled and cut into pieces that would be bite-sized for a baby

Directions:

Mash banana and yogurt together and add peach pieces, stirring until completely coated. Roll in ground oatmeal until the peach pieces are coated and easy to pick up.

Pick Up Cinnamon Sweet Potatoes

Ingredients:

- 1 sweet potato
- Ground cinnamon to taste

Directions:

Bake at 400 degrees F the sweet potato. It must be soft. Remove the skin and cut into bite sized cubes. Sprinkle with cinnamon to taste and have baby pick up and eat.

Tofu Cubes

Ingredients:

- Crushed cereal, granola, crackers or wheat germ
- 1 package of firm tofu
- Selection of herbs or spices

Directions:

Cut tofu into bite-sized cubes. Toss with spices and crushed crackers or cereal. Keep in sealed bag in the refrigerator until it's time to eat the food.

Butternut Squash Ravioli

Ingredients:

- 1/2 c flour
- 3/4 c butternut squash, cooked and mashed
- 1/3 warm water
- 1/2 c semolina flour
- 1 tablespoon olive oil
- Pinch paprika

Directions:

Mix together the flours and add oil and water slowly, mixing this well with a food processor on low. It should make a ball of dough that isn't too dry (add water if it doesn't form a ball). Knead dough and put in two balls. Roll each ball of dough to be extremely thin and stir butternut squash and paprika together. Put squash in small blobs on one line of dough and put the second layer of dough on the top, pressing around dough to make blobs of squash stuck in dough. Cut around blobs to make raviolis. Cook raviolis in hot water until pasta is done. Cook just three to four at a time. Serve with tomato sauce or other veggie puree.

Chicken Fingers with Apples

Ingredients:

- 1/2 onion, small
- 1 cup ground chicken
- 1 egg yolk, beaten
- 1 med. carrot
- 1 apple
- 1/2 clove of garlic
- Pinch dry thyme
- 1/4 c fresh breadcrumbs
- Pinch black pepper

Directions:

Peel carrots and grate. Do the same with the apple, onion and garlic. Mix everything together with ground chicken and add beaten egg yolk, bread crumbs and spices. When mixed well, make into 8 small sausages and broil for 10 minutes per side. Cool and store in the freezer so you can use them for a long time.

Broccoli and Cheese Nuggets

Ingredients:

- 1 pkg cooked frozen broccoli, chopped up
- 1 1/2 c shredded cheddar cheese
- 1 c seasoned breadcrumbs
- 3 eggs

Directions:

Set oven to 375 degrees F. Coat a baking sheet with oil. Mix rest of ingredients together, mixing well. Add garlic powder, basil, pepper and/or oregano. Make balls or squares out of these nuggets. Put the shapes on a baking tray and cook in oven for 20-25 minutes. Make sure to flip nuggets after fifteen minutes. Serve room temperature to warm.

Vegetable and Cheese Nuggets

Ingredients:

- 1 c dried bread crumbs
- 2.5 tablespoons olive oil
- 1 c frozen broccoli florets
- 2.5 tablespoons water
- 1.5 c cheddar cheese, grated
- 1.5 teaspoons baking powder

Directions:

Set oven to 375 degrees F. Cook broccoli in water and drain. Chop broccoli into tiny pieces. Mix all the ingredients together and form into nuggets on a nonstick baking tray. Bake in oven for 20-25 minutes, turning the nuggets halfway through. Serve room temperature or warmed.

Tofu Nuggets

Ingredients:

- 1 package of firm tofu
- 2 tablespoons grated parmesan cheese
- Garlic powder, 1 pinch
- 1 c crushed cornflakes
- Egg yolk, well beaten

Directions:

Set oven to 350 degrees F. Cut tofu into bite sized pieces. Dip the pieces in egg and then into crushed cornflakes. Cover each piece completely. Put foil onto baking sheet and spray it with nonstick cooking spray. Bake for 20 minutes, flipping the nuggets after ten minutes.

Infant Meatballs

Ingredients:

- 1 cup minced ground beef
- 1/2 c mashed potatoes

Directions:

Set oven to 350 degrees F. Mix all ingredients together and roll into one inch or smaller balls. Put on cooking tray and bake for twenty minutes. Get rid of grease by drying them on a paper towel. Serve cooled.

Applesauce Muffins for Baby

Ingredients:

- 1/4 c soft butter
- 3/8 c applesauce
- 1/4 c sugar
- 1 egg or egg substitute
- 2 teaspoon baking powder
- 1 c flour
- Pinch of cinnamon

Directions:

Set oven to 200 degrees F. Mix butter and sugar together and then beat in the egg or egg substitute. Beat in applesauce. Put dry ingredients together and then add dry ingredients.

Put into muffin tins and bake until golden (about 15 minutes). Break into bite sized pieces for baby.

Zucchini and Cheese Savory Muffins

Ingredients:

- 2 eggs or egg substitute
- 1 teaspoon dried oregano
- 3/4 c milk
- 2 teaspoons baking powder
- 2/3 c olive oil
- 1 c whole wheat flour
- 1 c plain flour
- 1 grated zucchini, medium
- 3 tablespoons cheddar cheese

Directions:

Set oven to 450 degrees F. Mix eggs and milks together and then put in oil. Put dry ingredients together and mix wet and dry ingredients. It should seem lumpy. Stir in zucchini and oregano. Make twelve muffins in a muffin tin and sprinkle cheese on top. Bake for 20-25 minutes, then serve cool, broken up into baby's bite sized pieces.

Wheat Bagels for age One Year or more

This recipe contains honey so you need to serve it to babies of at least one year or more.

Ingredients:

- 1.5 c water at 100-115 degrees F (use a thermometer to measure)
- 2 c whole wheat flour
- 1 pkg yeast
- 2 c regular flour
- 1.5 tablespoons honey
- 1/2 teaspoon salt

Directions:

Mix yeast, honey and water in a bowl and let sit for five minutes. Stir the flour and salt into yeast mixture and form a ball. Knead the ball on a floured surface for ten minutes or until the ball is smooth and elastic. Put ball in greased bowl and cover with cloth. Allow it to rise for an hour. Divide dough into ten pieces and shape into balls. Rest them for fifteen minutes and then mix 2 tablespoons of sugar in a large saucepan of water. Boil the water. Roll dough into a sausage and make into a circle, connecting the two ends with a bit of water. Boil bagels in boiling water for 4 minutes, flipping them after two minutes. Remove each bagel and dry with a paper towel very gently. Bake them on a greasy baking sheet for 20-25 minutes or until golden brown. Split and toast, adding butter or cream cheese to top of toasted bagel.

Pasta Stars with Tomato Sauce

This recipe takes sweet vegetables and mixes them with tomato sauce along with small stars or alphabet shapes for picking up. This is a recipe perfect for babies who are 9-12 months of age.

Ingredients:

- 1/2 small onion, chopped
- 1-2 heaping pasta stars
- 1 tablespoon olive oil
- 1 can (14 oz) crushed tomatoes
- 1 teaspoon brown sugar
- 1 tablespoon tomato paste
- 1/4 peeled, deseeded butternut squash
- 1 grated carrot, peeled
- 1/2 c vegetable stock
- Pinch of pepper
- 1 tablespoon Cheddar cheese

Directions:

Heat the oil in a frying pan and sauté the onion, carrot and squash until they are softened, about 3-4 minutes. Add tomatoes, vegetable stock, sugar and tomato paste. Boil this mixture and then let simmer for 40 minutes. Add pinch of pepper. Puree the tomato mixture and freeze in individual portions. When serving, take out a portion of tomato sauce and mix with prepared, cooked pasta. Stir in cheese when warm.

Little Salmon Fishcakes

Ingredients:

- 1 medium potato
- 3 tablespoons grated Parmesan cheese
- 5 ounces salmon
- 1 beaten egg
- 1 tablespoon mayo
- 4 tablespoons dry bread crumbs
- 1 tablespoon ketchup
- 2 tablespoons flour
- 2 large scallion, chopped finely
- 5 tablespoons of sunflower oil

Directions:

Poach salmon in simmering water until cooked completely—about 10 minutes. Remove and drain on paper towel. Put the potato in microwave and cook until soft. Let sit until you can touch it and peel off the skin with a knife. Mash potato in a bowl and flake salmon, removing any skin or bones. Mix potatoes and fish and add scallions, mayo and ketchup. Make small balls out of salmon mixture. Toss balls with flour and then egg and then in a mixture of Parmesan cheese and dried bread crumbs. Fry in oil until golden brown—about four minutes. Dry on paper towels and cool before serving.

Sweet Potato Fries

Ingredients:

- 6 medium sweet potatoes
- Oil for frying

Directions:

Set oven to 400 degrees F. Scrub sweet potatoes and peel if skins are tough. Cut into fries and coat with ¼ cup oil. Put in baking pan and drizzle remainder of oil onto fries. Bake in oven for 45 to 50 minutes. Alternately you can fry them in oil, cool and serve to baby or toddler.

Banana Pancakes

Ingredients:

- 2 ripe bananas
- Organic pancake batter

Directions:

Coat sliced bananas in pancake batter. Fry the coins lightly in a bit of oil, flipping halfway through, until they are golden brown. Serve warm.

Poached Salmon for Babies

This food is rich in omega-3 antioxidants. Because it breaks into big flakes, it's a good finger food. It's high in protein, iron, selenium, vitamin A and vitamin E. It's best for babies 9-12 months old.

Ingredients:

- 2 c vegetable stock
- 1 piece salmon, skin included, about 5 ounces

Directions:

Pour the stock into a saucepan and simmer. Add salmon with the flesh side down, simmering for 7 minutes. Cook after flipping another 3 minutes. It should be cooked through. Put salmon on a plate and peel off skin. Break into flakes to serve.

Chicken Balls

Poaching chicken makes it less chewy as a finger food. They can be served with organic tomato sauce. The recipe is high in protein, zinc, iron, calcium, selenium, folate, vitamin D and vitamin C and was designed for babies 9-12 months of age.

Ingredients:

- 3 cups chicken stock
- 1 diced shallot
- 1/4 teaspoon fresh thyme leaves
- 1 teaspoon olive oil
- 3 tablespoons grated Parmesan cheese
- 1 cup ground chicken
- 1/4 sweet apple, peeled and grated
- 1/3 c fresh bread crumbs
- Pepper to taste

Directions:

Sauté shallot in oil until soft. Cool in food processor for five minutes. To processor, add the rest of the ingredients and process the whole thing. Roll into small balls. Poach in chicken stock in saucepan until chicken is cooked through. Let cool on paper towels and add tomato sauce if desired.

Turkey Sticks with Applesauce

Ingredients:

- 1 pound ground turkey
- Pinch of basil
- 1/4 c bread crumbs
- 1 egg
- 1/2 c pureed carrots
- 1/4 c oat bran
- 1/4 c applesauce
- Pinch of garlic powder

Directions:

Put ground turkey in large bowl and add rest of ingredients, mixing well. Add more applesauce if it seems too dry and more oat bran if it seems too moist. Put mixture in oiled loaf pan and bake with foil covering pan at 350 degrees F for about 45 minutes. Slice into logs or crumble into pieces. You can make them into turkey sticks and bake in baking sheet until cooked through.

Tofu Nuggets

Ingredients:

- 1 package of firm tofu
- 1 teaspoon paprika
- 2 egg yolks
- 1 c fine cracker or bread crumbs
- 1/4 c flour
- 1 teaspoon garlic powder
- 1 dash pepper

Directions:

Set oven to 350 degrees F. Cut tofu into cubes. Put flour on plate and beat eggs onto another plate or dish. Put rest of ingredients in shallow dish. Coat each piece in flour, then into the egg yolks, and then into the rest of the ingredients. Bake at 350 degrees F for 15-20 minutes. Tofu will be crisp. Serve with a dipping sauce like pureed fruit or ketchup.

Conclusion

Babies change. They change in size, they change in their motor development and they change in terms of the food you feed them. And that change happens fast. Babies are only exclusively fed formula or breast milk for six months. During that time, they evolved from a helpless newborn to a baby that can sit up, hold its head up and open its mouth in response to a spoonful of food. It becomes time for a big change in the baby's life and an explosion of different foods for its palate.

Babies start the process of weaning to solid foods by consuming an organic cereal that is pureed and mixed with baby formula or breast milk. After a few days, try feeding the baby an organic vegetable that has been pureed and thinned out so it's really thin. Most pediatricians recommend waiting 3-4 days before changing foods so as to make sure the baby isn't allergic to the food you're feeding her.

After trying a few vegetables, you begin trying single fruits. Once your baby tolerates a variety of fruits and vegetables, you can feed the baby mixed foods or at least more than one kind of food each meal. Pediatricians recommend feeding the baby solid foods 2-3 times per day and using breast milk or formula in between. Much of the time, you can select times for feeding baby when the entire family is eating. This involves the baby in the family meal process and it becomes easier later on to take pieces of food from the family meal and puree or mash them into baby's bite-sized pieces.

We hope this book has convinced you that organic food is the best choice for your baby. It has more nutrition in it and is free of pesticides, chemicals and hormones. Organic foods are simply better for you and for your child. The fewer chemicals in the baby's food, the better the food is for baby. By feeding your baby organic food, you are starting your baby's eating habits on the right foot.

After fruits and vegetables, you can feed your baby meats and pasta. Some babies refuse pureed meat; however, when mixed with fruits or vegetables, it makes for a complete meal. You can even grind pasta with your meat and vegetables to have a perfect "casserole" for your baby.

Some babies will have allergies to dairy products, nuts, eggs and other foods. By feeding each food to baby individually at first, you can find out what they are allergic to and avoid it. Babies tend to outgrow many allergies so you should talk to your pediatrician about when to try feeding the baby or toddler the food again. Some allergies can be outgrown by 12 months of age.

You will also be transitioning your baby from the bottle to the cup, beginning at six months and completing the process at around 12 months of age. The baby will be eating more food during that time in their life so there will be less liquid food. The baby will probably have between 2 and 4 8-ounce sippy cups a day, either with a meal or between meals. Your baby can have juice, preferably diluted to reduce sweetness, along with a couple of sippy cups full of whole milk. Pediatricians recommend whole milk until the age of two because the baby needs the milk fat to grow. After that, talk to your pediatrician about what milk to feed your toddler.

Eventually, your baby will grow out of baby food and into toddler food. Toddler food resembles adult food more and there will be more food for your toddler to pick up because she often refuses to be spoon fed and can't spoon food in her mouth in ways that make for robust nutrition. This is why the list of recipes included finger food.

There is included a chapter on baby food and finger food. Baby food doesn't have to come from a jar and can be made from organic ingredients to be the right consistency and flavor for your baby. Many of the recipes included salmon, which provides healthy omega 3 fatty acids, vitamins and minerals that really can't be found in jarred baby food. This type of fish can be flaked and eaten alone or mixed with vegetables and formed into sticks or balls after cooking.

Toddlers can be fed food with spices in them, including thyme, coriander and pepper. It is not recommended to salt the baby's food because this gives the baby the taste for salt and won't tolerate less salted foods. We, as Americans, are eating too much salt in our diets the way it is. It's a good idea to start out with foods that are flavored less with salt and more with other healthy spices.

If your baby was premature or has special needs, talk to your pediatrician about what foods to feed your baby and when to start feeding the baby. For example, some foods aren't started until 17 weeks after the baby's due date. This means that preterm babies start eating solid foods when their chronological age is older than babies who were born at term.

Baby food is designed to be wholesome, palatable and an adventure for the baby. This can easily be achieved, not by expensive low nutrition jarred food but by organic baby food that can be made in batches and stored in individual portions through putting the recently prepared food in ice cube trays. Once the food is frozen, it can be stored in freezer bags so your baby can enjoy it for days after it was prepared.